colour me!

CREATE YOUR OWN confidence

Published by Collins
An imprint of HarperCollins Publishers
Westerhill Road, Bishopbriggs,
Glasgow G64 2QT

www.harpercollins.co.uk
HarperCollins Publishers
Macken House,
39/40 Mayor Street Upper,
Dublin 1
D01 C9W8
Ireland

Illustrations © Clare Forrest
Text © Becky Goddard-Hill

978-0-00-854521-5

Printed in Italy

10 9 8 7 6 5 4 3 2 1

Internal images on pages 8, 9, 10, 21, 23, 26, 56-57, 65, 70-71, 79, 80,
82-83, 97 and 140-141 © Shutterstock.com

With thanks to Michelle I'Anson, Lauren Murray,
Kevin Robbins, Gordon MacGilp, Rebecca Jones
and the whole team at Harper Collins for guiding,
designing and producing this gorgeous book and
for always supporting children's confidence and
wellbeing through their work. A huge thank you,
too, to Clare Forrest for her beautiful, thoughtful
drawings.

This book is dedicated to Jonny, Frankie and Annalise
for always listening to my ideas and having infinite
confidence in me.

#CYOConfidence

CREATE YOUR OWN confidence

Becky Goddard-Hill

illustrated by Clare Forrest

Being confident means believing in yourself and trusting yourself. It means feeling able to give things a go and not losing faith in yourself even if they don't work out.

Being confident makes everything feel easier, from making new friends to facing your fears.

Confidence isn't something you have to be born with though. It comes from the thoughts you think and the actions you take. Even if you aren't confident right now, the good news is you can learn how to be.

About this book

This book will help you create your own confidence with activities such as power posing, drawing, speaking, creating a confidence squad, designing a control wheel and even making paper! You will have lots of fun learning how to be more confident as you work through the activities.

Each topic contains:

- An inspiring quote to motivate you and get you thinking.
- Science or research that explains how the confidence strategy works.
- An activity to help you put what you have learned into practice.

Sections

The activities in this book will help you learn how to be confident in lots of different situations and lots of different ways, even when it might seem tricky.

Each section is packed with ways to help you be more confident through all areas of your life both now and in the future.

How to use this book

You can dip into the book and just read a topic at a time or you can zoom through it all. You can start with your trickiest area or work through it in order. It is your confidence journey so it is entirely up to you.

You may want to involve your grown-up or do some of the activities with a friend. Maybe you want to keep it private - the choice is yours.

Do have a go at all the activities, no matter how unusual they seem, because the best way to become confident is to take action. You never know what will work best for you until you give it a try.

Creating your own confidence will take effort and practice but it will change your life for the better and it will make you happier. Have fun!

colour me!

SELF CONFIDENCE

1. Unique, wonderful you

By being yourself, you put something wonderful in the world that was not there before.

— Edwin Elliot

It can feel safe to be just like everyone else: liking the same music, wearing the same clothes, having the same opinions, and being interested in the same things. It can make you feel more comfortable to feel you don't stand out.

Deep down though, you know that you aren't exactly like everyone else, and you have your own thoughts, feelings, interests and more. All of these combined make you absolutely original and rather amazing!

Did you know that every single snowflake and every single fingerprint is also absolutely unique? And that there are 8 billion people in the world and only one you?

When you value and enjoy the things that make you special it boosts your confidence, and you begin to respect and value the differences you see in others. Try complimenting them on the things that make them different, and give their confidence a boost too.

How it works

The mental health charity Mind has discovered that confidence comes from two things:

1 *Believing in yourself, your abilities, and ideas*

2 *Understanding and accepting yourself for who you are*

Confidence doesn't come from fitting in, it comes from knowing and liking who you really are.

Activity: Create an all-about-me collage

Using magazines, newspapers and any other bits and bobs you can find, make a poster or journal that explores everything about you. Display it with pride and look at it often – be proud of the only you on this entire planet.

As an extra activity you might like to watch or read *Wonder* by R. J. Palacio. It is a wonderful book that tells the story of a boy who is very different from his peers and how he learns to accept this.

Create your own confidence...

...by being your true self.

2. Perfectly imperfect

Have no fear of perfection; you'll never reach it.
                              - Salvador Dali

Working hard, doing your best and being enthusiastic will all get you closer to your goals, but they don't guarantee perfect results.

Sometimes things go wrong no matter how hard you try: cakes can sink if someone opens the oven door, and excellent goalies will sometimes save your best strikes.

How it works

If you are only happy when things are perfect, then you are going to be disappointed and upset regularly (or exhausted!).

You can always control the effort and energy you put into something, but you cannot always control the outcome.

Next time something doesn't go 100 percent your way, try these tips...

1 Be kind to yourself. Would you tell a friend they're rubbish at football?

2. Look at what went well. Perhaps the cake tasted amazing, even if it looked a little wonky.

3. Focus on the learning. Look to grow from imperfect results rather than considering them a failure.

Activity: Make yourself laugh

Put a pen in the hand you don't usually write with. Give yourself 1 minute to draw a picture of yourself upside down.

Now look at your picture – did it make you laugh?

Of course, it isn't perfect, but I bet it was fun. The quality of your drawing is not what matters. If you had a good time doing it and had an interesting and new experience, then it was worthwhile. Achievement isn't everything. You can find meaning and joy in every experience that doesn't work out perfectly.

Create your own confidence...

...by trusting you can cope, even if things don't go to plan.

If you do what you love, it is the best way to relax.
- Christian Louboutin

Circle the things you love to do below.

skateboarding

dance

read

WRITE

MAGIC

PLAY FOOTBALL

sing

CLIMB

DRAW

swim

go to scouts

cycle

gymnastics

walk your dog

KNIT

run

play the piano

Hobbies are good for you.

A study in New Zealand found that taking part in creative activities can lead to an improved sense of wellbeing that lasts for days! Some doctors even prescribe hobbies instead of medicine to people who are struggling with low mood.

How it works

When you do a hobby you love, you will often get into a 'state of flow' which means you are completely absorbed in what you are doing, not distracted by, or thinking of, anything else.

This is sometimes called *being in the moment.* It is relaxing for your brain because you can't worry about the past or what's happening tomorrow when you are in the moment.

Hobbies help your confidence

Hobbies might make your body stronger, or teach you about teamwork, time management, losing and winning. They might make your craft skills better and you might learn a new skill. You benefit so much from hobbies.

With most hobbies, the more you practise them the more able you become. This is great for your confidence.

Hobbies let you be you

Hobbies are a chance to express who you are and what you are uniquely interested in.

It might be tempting to go to street dance because all your friends are, and you want to fit in, BUT if hockey makes your heart sing and gives you the biggest smile then grab your courage and go for that instead. You will soon make new friends who like the same things you do, and it can be really good to socialise with other people outside of your school circle and have something separate.

Activity: Make time for hobbies

Screen time might be lots of fun but there is a MASSIVE world of hobbies out there and the boost to your happiness, confidence and self-esteem means they are well worth exploring.

1. Look at your favourite hobby and list five ways it benefits you.

2. Now have a think about something new you would love to try. Bagpipes, magic tricks, origami, French cricket, perhaps? Let your imagination run wild. How can you make that happen? Can you do some research?

Create your own confidence...

...by finding a few hobbies that make you feel great!

4. Love yourself

You are your best thing.
                              - Toni Morrison

What do you love about yourself?

Maybe it's your talents, your skills, your curly hair
or your brilliant smile? Loving good things about
yourself and knowing what they are is called
having high self-esteem. It goes hand-in-hand
with confidence.

Self-love is different.

What is self-love?

Self-love is when you value, accept and take care of all of yourself: your body, your mind and all of your feelings.

Here are some examples of self-love:

1. Self-love is knowing your brain needs a break from studying so you go out into the garden.

2. It's knowing your body is tired from gymnastics so you take a long bath.

3. It's when you leave a friendship behind because you keep being teased.

4. Self-love is when you ask for help because you keep getting angry and losing control.

5. It's saying to yourself, 'I can do this' when you need encouragement.

6. It's being the best friend you could ever be – to yourself.

7. Self-love is loving yourself through good times, hard times, sad times, frustrating times and in fact ALL the time.

How it works

Professor Kristin Neff at Texas University in America has researched self-love and found that it has many benefits. It has been found to encourage people to try again when they fail and helps them feel less stressed. This is because the kindness and care that self-loving people show themselves encourages them and soothes them.

Self-love is powerful and knowing that you always have someone on your side will increase your confidence.

Activity: A self-love meditation

Give yourself some love by trying this simple meditation:

- Find a comfortable position and close your eyes.

- Breathe in through your nose for a count of 4, hold for 4 and then breathe out through your mouth for a count of 4. Do this 4 times.

- Now place your hand on your heart and say the following to yourself:

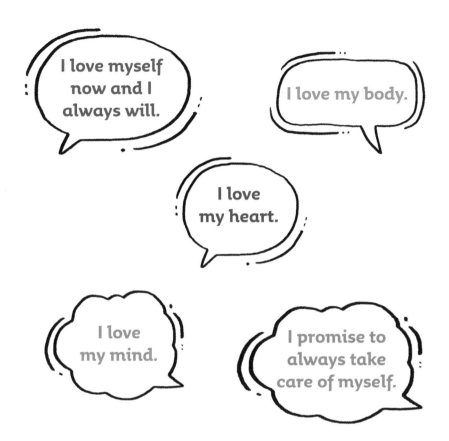

I love myself now and I always will.

I love my body.

I love my heart.

I love my mind.

I promise to always take care of myself.

● Tap your heart one last time and smile. Feel the warmth of your smile spread through your body from the top of your head to the tips of your toes.

Do this whenever you need a self-love top up.

Create your own confidence...

...by giving yourself some self-love.

5. Being a confident learner

A 'genius' is often merely a talented person who has done all of his or her homework.

- Thomas Edison

Perhaps you find art easy, but maths makes you want to scream. Or you can do tricky sums but trying to catch a ball can end in disaster, no matter how hard you try. Research has shown that confident students achieve more, are happier, and are more successful.

How it works

Confident learners (those who know they will get there in the end) do these three things:

1 They practise

When you learned to read you probably struggled before you could do it. Because you practised these skills again and again you got there in the end. Some things take a lot of learning, but once learned they feel so easy.

2   They have a 'can-do' attitude

When you tell yourself 'I can't do science' or 'It's too hard', you will begin to lose confidence, feel frustrated and stop trying.

BUT if you think 'I can do science' and 'I can try my best', your thoughts will be positive, you will FEEL confident and in control, and so you will ACT differently, practising more, working harder, and getting help if you need it.

A 'can-do attitude' makes ALL THE DIFFERENCE.

3   They Ask!

Asking for help when you need it stops you getting stuck and confused in your learning. Speak up. Teachers want you to do well and you can't learn what you don't understand!

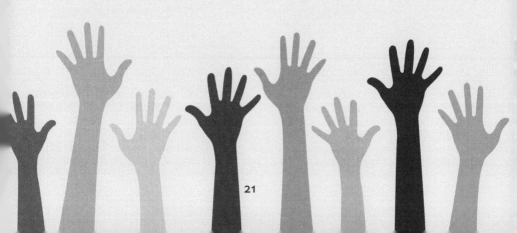

Activity: Create an achievement log

You learn things successfully every single day so you should certainly have confidence in your ability to learn.

This week, focus on at least one thing you have learnt and understood each day (no matter how small).

Either write it up in your journal each night or share it at the dinner table. You could ask your grown-up what they learned today too?

Do this for seven days and focus on how fabulous you are at learning!

Create your own confidence...

...by having a great attitude, practising, and asking for help.

Monday

Tuesday

Wednesday

Thursday

Friday

Saturday

Sunday

6. You are strong

Promise me you'll always remember: You're braver than you believe, and stronger than you seem, and smarter than you think.

- A. A. Milne

Sometimes, if things are going wrong or you are feeling sad or fed up it can be easy to forget that you are strong and you can cope.

Knowing what your strengths are and how they can help you can be so useful in times like that.

How it works

Looking at our strengths makes us feel far better about ourselves than if we only focus on what we find hard.

Studies have found that both knowing and using our strengths leads to an increase in self-belief, self-esteem, self-acceptance and self-confidence.

Let's take a look at your strengths. Can you identify your strengths from the list of 50 on the next page? Try and circle at least ten!

honest
gentle
lively
optimistic

caring
curious

good at building
organised

artistic
self-controlled
a leader

loyal
sweet
wise
funny

fast
tidy
inspiring

fair
warm

helpful
assertive

intelligent
a team player

brave

hard-working
logical
flexible

patient
thoughtful

kind
adventurous
musical

courageous

trustworthy
confident

determined

fun
inclusive

sensitive
(you don't leave
anyone out)

resilient
(able to bounce back
when things go wrong)

friendly

good at remembering

a good problem solver

giving
full of ideas

energetic
sporty

considerate
(thinking of others)

independent

Now have a go at answering the questions below using the strengths you have circled on the previous page.

1 The strengths you use in friendships are...

_____

_____

2 The strengths that help you in class are....

_____

_____

3 And at break times...

_____

_____

4 At home, what strengths do you use to get along with everybody?

_____

_____

5 When you do your favourite hobby, which of your strengths do you use?

_____

_____

The purpose of this activity is to show you just how many strengths you have and how they can help you out in lots of different situations if you put them to use. You are probably stronger and more capable than you first thought.

Are there any of the strengths in the list on the previous page that you find challenging, that you didn't circle, but would like to work on? If so, how are you going to do that? Write some ideas in the space below.

Create your own confidence...

...by recognising and using your strengths.

7. Quiet confidence

Never assume that loud is strong and quiet is weak.
- George Santayana

When you think about confident people you might imagine them to be loud, enthusiastic and always in charge. You might think people who are quiet and who don't often take the lead must be unconfident.

What you see on the surface (on the outside) of someone doesn't always reflect their inside. Loud people who look confident but aren't sometimes go to pieces when things go wrong or if they are criticised.

Sometimes it's the quiet people who are deeply confident, they just don't want to lead or be the decision-maker every time.

The centre of attention

People who need the light to shine on them are sometimes looking for other people to make them feel good, strong or important because they don't feel that way inside of themselves.

It does take confidence to speak up, make decisions and take charge of a team but sometimes people are faking it, hiding how unconfident they really are behind their noise.

Did you know…?

The Psychology Dictionary defines self-confidence as:

'An individual's trust in his or her own abilities, capacities and judgments, or belief that he or she can successfully face day-to-day challenges and demands.'

No mention of being the boss, getting others' approval, shouting loudly or being in the spotlight at all!

Confidence relies on you

Quietly confident people let other people into the spotlight too. They don't compare themselves to others and can listen without needing to always talk. Because they know they don't need anyone else's approval, they don't need to be boastful or show off.

Don't feel you have to act a certain way to show how confident you are... just be you: quiet, loud, funny, clever, down to earth, or silly. Confidence is about being yourself and knowing that you are good enough.

And, if you have a friend who is a bit boastful and shows off, know that inside they might feel unconfident and perhaps need some extra support.

Can you fill in the rest of this acrostic about what you think real confidence is...

C

O

NOT SCAREd TO TRY NEW THINGS

FIGHT FOR WHAT I BELIEVE IN

i

DON'T GIVE UP ON MY GOALS

E

N

C

E

Create your own confidence...

...by quietly trusting and believing in yourself.

8. Powerful you

Do not let what you cannot do interfere with what you can do.

— John Wooden

There are many things you can't control in life but there are many more things that you can.

Knowing what you can control helps you feel strong and powerful, and it boosts your confidence.

How it works

When we feel in control, the prefrontal cortex (the thinking part of our brain) takes charge and we can make clear decisions and think things through logically.

Studies have shown that when people don't feel in control, the emotional part of their brain (the amygdala) takes over and they can feel anxious, stressed and helpless.

This explains why people feel safer driving a car than flying in a plane (even though it's not safer). People feel better, happier and calmer when they are in control.

Look at all the items in the list below. Can you fill the inside of the wheel with all the things you can control and write the things you can't control around the outside of the wheel?

My choices   My attitude

Other people's actions   MY EFFORTS

My goals   Other people's thoughts

TAKING CARE OF MY BODY

My actions   Being a good friend

How people treat me   MY THOUGHTS

Making a difference

My self-care

OTHER PEOPLE'S OPINIONS

THE PAST   My beliefs

How I express my

THINGS THAT HAPPEN IN THE WORLD   feelings

Asking for help

THE WAY I TALK TO MYSELF

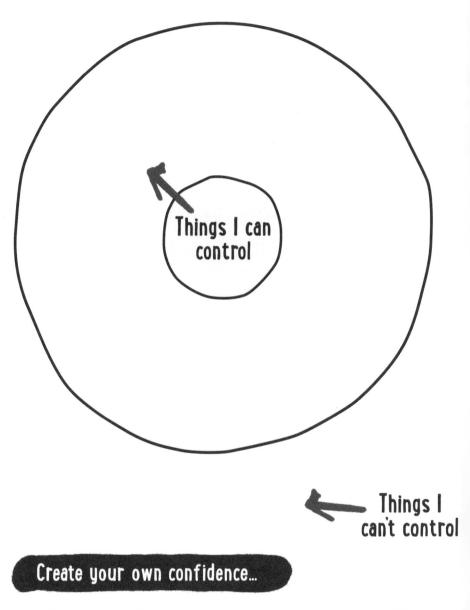

Things I can control

Things I can't control

Create your own confidence...

...by putting all your energy into the areas of your life you CAN control (and not worrying about the rest).

colour me!

FEELING CONFIDENT

9. Fear of failing

It's not how far you fall, but how high you bounce that counts.

- Zig Ziglar

Failing feels rubbish at first but it is your attitude towards it that affects how much it knocks your confidence.

What's the worst that can happen?

- If you suggest a game, your friends might not want to play it (but they might, and it could be brilliant).

- If you join a new club, you might not like it and perhaps you'll leave (but you might love it and make loads of new friends).

How a growth mindset helps

Thoughts like 'I can't do it', 'I'm rubbish at this' and 'This is too hard' come from a FIXED mindset, one that believes things can't change. This leads to feelings of low confidence and makes you want to give up.

Try swapping these phrases for 'I can't do this YET' and 'I can learn!'

These are growth-mindset phrases which encourage you to try again and build up your confidence. A growth mindset means you believe you can grow and learn and that with practice and effort you can achieve anything (or at least get better at it).

Activity: Be inspired

The Leaning Tower of Pisa wasn't supposed to be leaning, but if it were straight, it probably wouldn't be such a popular tourist attraction.

Wouldn't it be a shame if it had been knocked down just because it was seen as a failure?

Steven Spielberg was rejected both times he applied to attend film school. That didn't stop him. He has now directed more than 30 films.

Good job he didn't quit when things went wrong!

Create your own confidence...

...by being unafraid of failure and bouncing back with style.

10. Courage

You can choose to let this thing bother you or let this be an adventure and welcome the challenge.

\- Fred Rogers

Fear is an emotional reaction to something you see as a threat. It starts in the amygdala, the part of our brain that deals with emotion. It alerts our body to danger and tells it to release adrenaline, a hormone which makes our muscles tense up and our breathing get faster – so we are ready for 'fight or flight'.

This is useful if you are about to get munched by a lion on the loose.

Some fears are helpful because they keep us away from danger. But there are some fears that only exist in our imagination, and these aren't helpful. They make us tremble for no good reason, and can stop us from doing things that would be fun or rewarding.

These imagined fears might come from a story you have been told, or they may have been passed on to you by someone else. Or, they may be from just one single experience you've had that you worry will be repeated.

Let's imagine you are scared of ducks...

It may be because, once, a duck flapped at you, or because your sister thinks they are scary, or because you read a story about a naughty duckling when you were small.

This fear could stop you taking your dog for a walk by the river or crossing the local park by the pond because you are afraid you will see a duck there.

When fears interfere with your life it is time to face them. If you don't, your lack of confidence will only increase.

So, how can you be more courageous?

Identify what you are scared of then turn it into a goal

In this case, 'I am scared of ducks' (fear) would become: 'I will walk past ducks happily' (goal).

Try writing that goal in the middle of a page and surrounding it with great ideas that will help you reach it.

Every single tiny action you take to face the thing you are scared of will help your fear shrink and your confidence grow.

Get yourself a cuddly duck so you start thinking of them as cute.

Draw pictures of ducks so you get used to seeing them.

Watch duck videos on YouTube so you become curious.

Listen to music as you walk by some ducks.

Borrow a book about ducks from the library.

Ask a friend to walk past ducks with you.

Practise deep breathing before you walk past ducks.

Take your camera with you and take photos of the ducks.

Now you try it...

Activity: Face your fear

Turn one of your imagined fears into a goal and think of lots of ways that would help you reach that goal, then cross them off one by one as you do them.

Create your own confidence...

...by being brave and facing your fears.

11. Optimism

Believe you can and you're halfway there.
- Theodore Roosevelt

Being optimistic means you are pretty confident that things will work out okay. Being an optimist is a great thing to be...

- Optimists see opportunities instead of problems.
- Optimists think anything is possible with the right attitude and hard work.
- Optimists believe that, even in hard times, things will work out in the end.

How it works

Scientists believe that 25 percent of your optimism is down to genetics (which means it's passed down from your parents) or influenced by the world you grew up in. That leaves a massive 75 percent of your optimism within your control!

The benefits of optimism

Researchers have linked optimism to people having better physical and mental health, being less stressed, being happier and living longer.

Optimism doesn't mean bad things never happen because in life sometimes they will, but it does mean you know you will cope, that things do change and they will get better.

Activity: How to become more optimistic

Looking at all there is to be thankful for in your life helps you to see how full of good things it is. This can help you have confidence that the future will be good too.

Keeping a gratitude journal, where you write down three good things from your day, is a great way to capture these happy moments.

Create your own confidence...

...by being an optimist.

12. Confidence in hard times

Tough times never last, but tough people do!
                    - Robert Schuller

Sometimes life can be tough and your confidence in your ability to cope may wobble.

Everyone – yes, every single person on Earth – has hard times sometimes. Perhaps...

- someone you care about is ill
- you are being bullied
- your parents are separating
- someone you love has died.

Two things are important to remember when you are going through times like these:

1. Feeling unhappy sometimes is absolutely normal; it is part of being human.

2. Difficult situations will pass with time or when something changes. Hard times never last forever – even, if right now, it feels like they will.

Talk your worries over with someone you trust (not just someone you like). People who are calm and sensible will help you be calm and sensible too and they may be able to listen, support and advise you.

Let yourself feel what you feel and cry and shout if it helps (just not at other people). Burying emotions inside you will cause you lots of tension and will probably make you feel worse.

Look after yourself when things are hard. If you don't eat properly, sleep, exercise and keep yourself clean and healthy you will feel much worse. Treat yourself with love and care.

Name it to tame it

Dan Siegel is a psychiatrist who says that when you have a big, upsetting feeling you should 'Name it to tame it'. This is another way of saying label your feelings. When you describe your emotions with words, you kick start your thinking brain which then calms down the emotional part of your brain and puts you back in control.

Have confidence in your ability to cope: gather up your courage, optimism and support, feel your feelings and express them, look after yourself and keep a cool head.

You will get through these hard times, you will cope.

Sometimes when life is tough you may feel you cannot do a great deal to change things, but you can always lift your mood...at least a little.

Circle the things that work for you from the list below. You might even want to make your own list.

Hugs   A warm drink

Baking   A long bath

Lying in the grass   Playing a board game

Playing outside   Watching a movie

Sunshine

Being in the garden   Walking the dog

Create your own confidence...

...by taking care of yourself when times are tough.

13. Determination

Some people dream of success... while others wake up and work hard at it.

— Unknown

The definition of determination is 'the ability to continue trying to do something, even if it is difficult'. Let me tell you a true story...

George is 12 and lives in Scotland. When he was 4, his parents started taking him to swimming lessons.

The pool George went to had 8 different levels that you had to work through. By level 8 you needed to be able to do the breaststroke, backstroke, front crawl and tumble turns (where you spin underwater at the end of one length and push off against the side of the pool to start your next).

By the age of 10, George had made it through levels 1 to 7. He was a fantastic swimmer. He even won races at his school carnival.

But there was one thing that George couldn't do... tumble turns. After TWO YEARS, George was still stuck on level 7.

But George was determined. He decided to be creative and try something different. He went to a gymnastics class, and told the teacher that he needed help learning to do tumbles on a soft mat, so that maybe he could do them better in the pool. After just one class, George went back to swimming and managed to do his first ever tumble turn. By the end of the lesson, he'd managed to do loads!

Everyone was proud of him but most importantly, George was proud of himself. He'd worked so hard and finally achieved his goal.

Recent research suggests that having determination is more important than being smart when it comes to being successful. Luckily your determination is something you can control.

Activity: Be determined

Think of something you would like to achieve and promise yourself to 'be like George' and give it your all. Write your pledge on a scrap of paper and keep it somewhere safe.

Create your own confidence…

…by being determined.

14. When your confidence gets knocked

When you are knocked down you have two choices: stay down or get back up, stronger.

- Alesha Dixon

Imagine it's a Monday morning and you head off to school with a smile, clutching your new cool water bottle and with hopes for making the football team.

'You didn't make the team,' Coach tells you after try-outs.

'You got 0/10,' says your teacher, handing back your test.

'Have you really lost your new water bottle?' says Dad crossly as you arrive home.

Some days life just knocks your confidence right out of you.

So, what can help?

Feel your feelings

It's okay to feel frustrated and annoyed when your confidence gets knocked. It's part of being human. Express how you feel and have a cry or moan if it helps. Keeping it inside will make you feel worse.

Keep some perspective

Remind yourself of the good things that happened. Did you draw a great picture in art? Did Leo invite you to his party? I bet it wasn't all bad.

Don't catastrophise (make something bigger than it is)

Getting no marks on your test simply means you need to revise harder or ask for help next time. It is only one test – don't let it become a bigger problem than it needs to be.

Make a plan

How can you plan to make things better? Maybe you could apologise to your dad and promise to hunt for the bottle tomorrow? Or try out for rugby instead?

Just because things have gone wrong doesn't mean they have to stay wrong.

Bounce back

Now you have worked through your disaster day you can let it go and do something relaxing and confidence-boosting instead.

Activity: Yogurt pot cakes

This recipe is super simple and it always works! You will need:

- 1 pot of your favourite yogurt
- 1 potful of sunflower oil (use the empty yogurt pot as a measure)
- 1 potful of caster sugar
- 3 potfuls of self-raising flour
- 3 eggs
- Chopped fresh strawberries or raspberries or even choc chips (optional)

Put all the ingredients into a bowl and mix well.

Divide the mixture between 12 muffin cases and bake for 20 minutes at 180 °C or 160 °C fan.

Create your own confidence…

…by helping yourself feel good again.

CONFIDENT THOUGHTS

colour me!

15. Know your worth

You yourself, as much as anybody in the entire universe, deserve your love and affection.

- Buddha

Your self-esteem is your opinion about yourself. When you have low self-esteem you might compare yourself to others, worry about upsetting people, feel unlikeable and perhaps helpless if things go wrong.

Low self-esteem can make you feel rubbish.

If you have high self-esteem you don't think you are PERFECT but you do know that when things go wrong you can cope and bounce back. You know that people are happy to help you and find you likeable. You also know you don't need to compare yourself to others because you are wonderful in your own way.

High self-esteem means you like, respect and trust yourself and this makes life much easier.

How it works

Researchers have discovered that high self-esteem makes people happier in their work, in their friendships and in their mental health.

They also found that those with high self-esteem cope better with their problems because, rather than getting stuck, they trust themselves to change things if they can and to cope if they can't.

High self-esteem is a great thing to have and it's worth working on!

How to raise your self-esteem

Looking at your strengths and recognising how wonderful you are takes practice, but if you do this regularly your self-esteem will rise. You never have to wait for someone else to tell you that you are fabulous – you can do that yourself.

The activity below helps you know your worth and if you're ever having a self-esteem wobble you can either repeat the activity or read over your answers to boost yourself up again.

Activity: The self-esteem interview

Have a go at interviewing yourself by answering the questions in the spaces provided. This is YOUR confidence journey, so you get to choose.

- I love the way I...

- I am clever at....

- I feel happy when I...

- These people really care about me:

_____

- I coped well when...

_____

- I am good at...

_____

- My friends like me because I...

_____

- I am proud of myself because I...

_____

- I can make people laugh by...

_____

- I have a talent for...

_____

- I get compliments for...

_____

- I like myself because I...

_____

Create your own confidence...

...by keeping your self-esteem high.

16. Decisions

Life is the sum of all of your choices.

— Albert Camus

Do you find it easy to make decisions?

When you feel confident, decisions are not so tricky. You weigh up what you think is the best choice and go for that (knowing that if it doesn't work out you will be okay).

If you are not feeling confident, decisions can seem like too much responsibility and can make you nervous.

If you find decision-making hard, here are six things that can help:

- Think about what your goals are.
- Ask for advice if you need it.
- Gather information to help you choose.
- Listen to your gut/your instinct/your heart.
- Calm yourself down before you decide.

And the golden rule of decision-making: practise, practise and practise again.

Some people are so worried about making a wrong decision that they suffer from *decidophobia*, or the fear of making decisions.

If you keep saying, 'I don't mind' or always let someone else choose, you will never learn to trust yourself. Trusting yourself is the key to confidence.

When you trust your own decisions you don't just follow what your friends do, or make the easiest choices, or do nothing…no, you do what you believe is right for YOU.

And if your decision ends up not being the perfect choice? Well, that's okay because you know by now that you can cope and you can either try again or try something else.

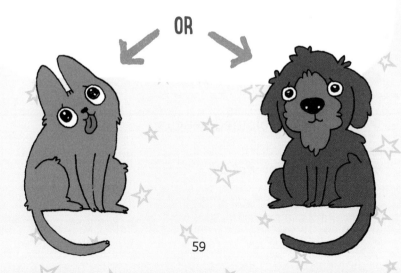

Activity: Let's make some decisions

I am going to ask you to make 20 decisions now and I want you to do it as quickly and confidently as you can. Calm yourself first with some deep breaths and then dive on in!

Do you prefer....

- milk or juice?

- pitta or toast?

- ice cream or cake?

- TV or YouTube?

- skating or swimming?

- new shoes or a new T-shirt?

- hot choc or chocolate?

- adventure or a mystery?

- felt tips or coloured pencils?

- lemonade or water?

Would you rather be...

- be sad or angry?

- be content or excited?

- be with new friends or old friends?

- read a book or listen to music?

- go to the shops or to the cinema?

- have a party or a big gift?

- tell on someone or have them pick on you?

- have toothache or see the dentist?

- learn to be confident or stay unconfident?

- learn to make choices or stay undecided?

Some choices are easy to make and some are hard but the more you practise, the clearer and more confident you will be.

Create your own confidence...

...by practising your decision-making.

17. Live your dreams

Don't dream your life, but live your dream.
- Mark Twain

What do you dream of being able to do but hold back on?

Maybe you would like to go for a part in the school play... or maybe you dream of one day being a vet or a published author?

Whatever your dream is, it doesn't need to stay just a dream. You can do a great deal towards making it happen.

If you want to get a part in the school play, you don't need to wait until you are confident enough to audition. Instead, increase your confidence by preparing well.

- Let your teacher know you are interested and ask for some tips.
- Rehearse your lines again and again.
- Practise singing along to the songs.
- Role play the part you are auditioning for with a friend.

- Watch the movie of the play several times.
- On audition day calm your nerves with some deep breathing and a power pose (read more about this on page 104) before you go on.

Preparation is key and will help you feel more confident when you try out for anything!

If you want to be a vet when you are older, that needn't be just a dream, something you might be 'lucky to have come true'. There is a lot you can do to help make it a reality.

- Read books on what being a vet is like.
- Study hard at school, especially in science and maths.
- Watch lots of animal documentaries on YouTube and TV.
- Visit friends who have various pets and find out all about them.
- Volunteer to help out in a vets or at an animal shelter or rescue centre once you are old enough.
- Look after school pets in the holidays.

Hard work and effort really pay off when it comes to building the confidence to go after your dreams.

And if your dream is to be a published author?

You could...

- read a lot and see what inspires you
- try writing in different genres (themes)
- try writing poetry
- have a go at short stories
- write a daily diary
- join a writing workshop
- plot your book!

You have to be determined and consistent when you want to become good at something.

With hard work, effort, determination, practice and preparation you are on your way to making your dreams come true.

Take action – don't wait to feel confident, instead build your confidence with your actions.

Write your dream in the dream space below.
What three things can you do to help it along?

Create your own confidence...

...by working towards your dreams.

18. Choose your focus

Where focus goes, energy flows.
                    - Tony Robbins

When you focus on something it gets bigger in your mind.

This is brilliant if you are focusing on something fantastic like a holiday, but becomes a problem if it's something you're worried about.

How it works

The Reticular Activating System (RAS) is a filter in your brain that lets in the things you are focused on and tells your brain to pay attention. That's why you will always see a spider if you're scared of them, even if no one else notices.

We find more of what we look for.

Choose what to think about

If I say think about a bad-tempered rabbit you'll probably frown.

But if I tell you to shout DELETE DELETE at the grumpy rabbit and instead imagine a multicoloured flying pony you will probably smile.

You can replace your thoughts at any time.

Activity: Change your focus

Quietly think about something you are feeling anxious or unconfident about and why.

Ask yourself what you want to achieve with this.

Be detailed about your goal and include how you want to feel. Write it down too. By focusing more on your goals than your concerns your brain will start noticing things that can help you, and your confidence will build.

Here's an example:

Negative focus
I am unsure if people will have a good time at my sleepover.

Positive focus
My goal is for my sleepover to be full of games and great snacks and we will all have fun and feel happy.

Now you have a go....

Negative focus

Positive focus

Create your own confidence...

...by changing your focus when it is not helping you.

19. Helpful thoughts

Once you replace negative thoughts with positive ones, you'll start having positive results.

— Willie Nelson

Some thoughts are not helpful.

Imagine you have a maths test...

If you think, 'I'm so bad at maths', you will feel worried, nervous and unconfident about your maths and during the test you are likely to not think clearly.

The unhelpful thought 'I'm so bad at maths' is making you feel and behave in ways that do not serve you very well.

Rather than concentrating on the test and thinking through your answers, these thoughts can you make you feel as though there's no point in trying in the first place.

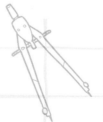

Imagine you have a maths test...

If you think, 'I can do my very best' or 'I will revise hard for this', you will feel confident and in control, and in your test you are more likely to feel calm and to think clearly.

These thoughts will be MUCH more helpful and will have a positive affect on your feelings and behaviour.

Practise turning your unhelpful thoughts to helpful thoughts. Think of a situation you're worried about below.

What I'm worried about

Unhelpful thoughts	Helpful thoughts

How it works

Thoughts change how you feel, and how you feel can change your behaviour. You can control your thoughts by telling the unhelpful ones to BE QUIET and listening to the helpful thoughts instead. This might take some practice at first.

Let's take a look at some annoying and unhelpful thoughts and how they can be replaced by helpful thoughts instead.

It's too hard	I can do hard things
I can't handle this	I can cope
I can't do this	I can do this
Everyone hates me	I have good friends
I'm so stupid	I learn new things all the time
I can't work this out	I can ask for the help I need

Unhelpful thoughts bash your confidence and helpful thoughts boost it, so always pick the helpful ones. This really does change everything.

Activity: Banish negative thoughts

Next time a negative thought comes into your head, I want you to write it down on a piece of paper then rip it into lots and lots of pieces and throw it away.

Do this a few times until you feel you can do it in your head without writing it down.

Remember: these thoughts don't help you.

You are the boss of your thoughts so give the unhelpful thoughts the shove.

Create your own confidence...

...by focusing on helpful thoughts.

20. Limiting beliefs

Life has no limitations, except the ones you make.
- Les Brown

Believing things about yourself that hold you back or stop you from achieving are called *limiting beliefs* (because they limit you). Examples include:

- 'I'm not good at making friends.'

- 'I'm a rubbish reader.'

- 'I'm not funny enough.'

Such thoughts may come from a mean comment someone has made. Or perhaps they have come from an event like not being invited to a party or being in the bottom reading stream.

It's hard to think straight when you are upset. This can lead to faulty thinking, where you start to believe untruths about yourself.

Limiting beliefs can take away your confidence. But thoughts are not facts. They are just thoughts, and you can change them.

Did you know…?

According to the National Science Foundation, you have 50,000 thoughts every day and 95 percent of them are repeated daily. If you think something negative about yourself repeatedly, it will affect how you act. Your beliefs need to encourage you, not hold you back.

Look for evidence

When a detective is trying to solve a case, they look for clues and search for proof. It's really helpful to try to do this when it comes to believing in yourself. First you need to flip that limiting belief you hold into a positive thought.

Let's practise…

Change the thought 'I am rubbish at making friends' into 'I can make new friends'.

Next, search for evidence that supports this:

- I have four good friends and they were all new once.
- I am warm and friendly.
- I always get asked to play at break time so people must like me.

You can make new friends – take your new belief and talk to someone new today.

Let's try it with reading...

Change 'I am a rubbish reader' into 'My reading is getting better and better'.

Search for evidence that supports this:

- I have read two books in the past week.
- I no longer just read books with pictures.
- My teacher says my reading has improved.

Your reading is getting better! Take your new belief and head to the library.

Activity: Become a confidence detective

Think about a negative thought you have about yourself and flip it into a positive statement. Then search for the evidence to support it.

Create your own confidence...

...by looking for evidence that supports your awesomeness.

ACTIONS

colour me!

21. Try new things

A comfort zone is a beautiful place but nothing ever grows there.

- Unknown

A comfort zone describes a place where you feel at ease and everything is familiar. New things can be scary BUT they can also be amazing. Stepping outside of our comfort zone brings new opportunities and experiences that can make life richer and more exciting.

Neophilia

Researchers have found that trying new things boosts both our physical and mental health. The wish for new experiences is called neophilia. People who practise *neophilia* have been found to live longer and happier lives.

Everything you now love – every hobby, friendship, taste or favourite place – was once new to you and if you hadn't moved out of your comfort zone these awesome things would not be in your life.

If you sit still it is hard to grow in confidence, in courage or in skills. Push yourself a little and see all of these things bloom as you do.

Maybe you want to be a famous artist one day. Joining that new workshop or trying that new style might just help you to reach your goal.

Activity: Step out of your comfort zone

Let's make life a daring adventure and try some new things. Can you fill in and action the following?

Something new I'm going to taste...

_____

Someone new I'm going to talk to...

_____

 A new hobby I am going to try...

_____

A new hairstyle I am going to try...

_____

Create your own confidence...

...and watch it grow as you try out new things.

22. Experimenting

You've got to experiment to figure out what works.
                                          - Andrew Weil

The best way to build confidence is to give things a go despite any worries you may have about messing up. When you experiment, there is always a little risk involved.

Did you know…?

In ancient times writing was done on plants, clay tablets, animal skins, wood material and stone walls. Then, 2,000 years ago, people in Egypt created a kind of paper from the papyrus plant. This is where the word 'paper' comes from.

In China in AD 105, a court official called Cai Lun began making paper using rags, plants and old fishing nets. Five hundred years later, people in Japan made paper with fibres of the mulberry tree.

Modern paper is normally made from wood, ground up and mixed with water and other chemicals.

Without all these experiments you wouldn't be able to read this! Do try things with confidence – experiments can lead to the most fantastic discoveries.

Activity: Make your own paper

1. Shred some paper – newspaper works well but any old paper will do.

2. Soak your paper in water for at least 30 minutes (though overnight is best).

3. Mash the paper into a pulp using your hands or a hand blender (with supervision).

4. Push the pulp into a sieve to remove the water.

5. Put it into a silk screen or pour into an empty large picture frame with greaseproof paper on the bottom.

6. Leave it to dry.

Create your own confidence by...

...being unafraid to try things out (but do, always, stay safe!).

23. Acts of kindness

We rise by lifting others.

— Robert Ingersoll

Being kind may sound like an odd way to boost your confidence, but it works (and in the process, makes someone else feel happy too).

Scientists have found that when you are kind to someone else the reward section in your brain lights up in just the same way as if someone had been kind to you.

Being kind feels good, and when you feel good about yourself you have more confidence in yourself too!

Acts of kindness and independence

Many acts of kindness require you to be responsible and act more independently.

Perhaps you...

- offer support to a younger child at school with their reading
- declutter your room and give some toys to a charity shop of your choice

- wash your mum's car on your own
- make a simple meal for your family.

Kindness activities like the ones above will help you to develop new skills and do more things by yourself. They might push you a little too, and when you accomplish them you will feel more confident in yourself and your abilities.

There are so many ways to be kind: you could give a compliment, help with chores, send your granny a letter, help your teacher tidy up, donate your pocket money to a good cause, look after your baby brother. What can you come up with?

Activity: A mug full of kindness

All you will need for this activity is a bag of pasta and a mug.

Whenever you do an act of kindness, put a piece of pasta into your mug. You can call this the kindness mug. Fill it up with pasta over the next few months and watch your confidence and trust in yourself bloom as you do.

Create your own confidence...

...by being kind.

24. Turning your 'I cant's' into 'I cans'

Whether you think you can, or you think you can't – you're right.

- Henry Ford

There are many things I can't do that I would like to be able to do:

I can't bring my grandad back to life.
I can't go back to being 6 again.
I can't ride a unicycle.

But I can put up photos of my lovely grandad and remember happy times with him.

I can play games from my childhood to remember how it felt to be 6.

I can learn to ride a unicycle, with a lot of practice.

See what I did there?

I turned my *I can'ts* into *I cans*. The 'I can'ts' made me feel a little sad and frustrated but the 'I cans' were much more positive. They made me feel happier and more excited.

How it works

Psychologist Angela Duckworth believes it is passion (being excited about what we want to achieve) and perseverance (hard work) that will lead us to success.

This is useful to know because these are things you can control. So if you want something, be happy, focus on your goal and get to work!

Activity: Yes you can!

Write down two things you can't do yet – one small thing and one big thing.

Using the list above, decide what you need in order to succeed at your small thing, then write your plan.

Now give it a go! When you have practised putting your 'I can' attitude to work and succeeded, give your big thing a go.

Create your own confidence...

...by switching your 'I can'ts' into 'I cans'.

25. When it's time for a change

Courage is the power to let go of the familiar.
— Raymond Lindquist

When people are confident, they seem to find changes such as moving to a new school or trying a new hobby exciting.

For people who aren't so confident, change can be scary, and they try to avoid it.

How do you feel about change?

Does it excite you or does it make you feel stressed and uncomfortable? Sometimes you might feel both. That's absolutely normal too.

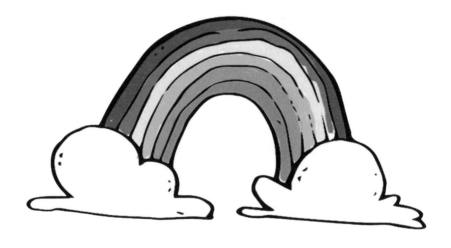

How it works

According to neuroscientists (brain experts), the brain really likes to know exactly what's happening in order to feel safe. Brains sometimes see changes as 'threats' or 'challenges' and this is why we feel anxious.

Let's look at what could help.

Talk about how you feel
Don't bottle up your worries, feelings or questions about the change ahead, this just makes you feel tense and nervous. Talk over how you feel, ask for support, and gather information to help you cope.

Imagine how it could go well
In times of change, it's easy for your mind to think about the worst things that can happen, but this isn't helpful.

Instead, visualise (imagine) how it could go well. Close your eyes and let the pictures form – see how this change could be brilliant. Your imagination is powerful and can affect how you feel, so use it to excite not scare you.

What can you see?

Think about the past
Remind yourself about changes you have coped with in the past that ended up working out well. Remember how many of your worries didn't come true.

Consider what you can control
Often change feels scary because you don't feel in control. But there is usually something you can control about the change. If, for example, you are changing schools, perhaps you could choose who you walk with, a new pencil case or the clubs you join?

A sense of control will ease your nerves.

Decide on a change that is coming up for you and start exploring.

If you are heading to a new school, do they offer a tour on their website?

If you are joining a new swimming team, could you watch a race before you start?

The more you know about the change ahead, the more prepared and confident you will feel.

What could you do?

_____

_____

_____

_____

_____

_____

Create your own confidence...

...by preparing yourself for change.

26. Confidence in your creativity

To live a creative life, we must lose our fear of being wrong.

— Joseph Chilton Pearce

When you were little you probably splattered paint everywhere, put all your playdough together to make crazy colours and always crayoned outside the lines.

You probably enjoyed your creativity every day without concern!

As people get older they start to be more aware of what other people think about what they create, and can lose confidence.

There are many brilliant reasons to be creative!

1. It's lots of fun.
2. It can take your mind away from any worries.
3. It is a way to express your feelings.
4. It can help you develop a particular skill.
5. It can change the way you look at things.

Lots of psychological studies have found that

when you are creative you can get into a state of flow where you are so deeply focused on what you are doing it leads to feelings of deep happiness and relaxation.

If you focus on being creative because you love it, you can be confident that it is worth it. How being creative makes you feel is far more important than the end result.

Activity: Throw away the rule book

The artist Pablo Picasso wasn't concerned about painting things that looked like the things they were supposed to. Have a look at some of his art. He tried to show an object from lots of different angles all at once using cube-like shapes. This style is called Cubism.

Another artist, Claude Monet, also didn't paint things that looked exactly as they were – instead, he used lots of short brush strokes to create an impression of what he saw. Have a look at his water lily paintings. They are gorgeous!

Create your own confidence...

...by making, creating, exploring and expressing YOUR way.

27. (You can) make a difference to the planet

Act as if what you do makes a difference. It does.
- William James

Sometimes the tiniest of actions can be super powerful and have varied, long-term benefits. When you plant wildflower seeds you make the world look prettier. You are also providing insects with shelter and food from leaves, pollen and nectar. In autumn, wildflowers drop their seeds, which will either be carried away by the birds and dropped or simply grow where they land. Your wildflowers will spread far and wide and multiply.

How it works

Every action you take may inspire someone to do something similar, which could in turn inspire someone else. For example, if you started a free bookstall outside your home, someone may take a book, think 'What a great idea!' and start a bookstall outside their home.

What you do to help the planet has much more impact than you might imagine. Have confidence that you can make a difference and take positive action to look after the planet and help it bloom.

Activity: Make an egg box bird feeder

Bird feeding is a good thing to do all year round but it is most important in late winter or early spring, when natural seeds are scarce. Birds might go hungry then, so let's give them a hand and make them a feeder.

1. Cut the flat top off an egg box and pop it in the recycling bin. (If you are vegan you might want to use a margarine carton or hummus pot.)

2. Punch holes in each corner of the box.

3. Tie string through the hole in each corner and then gather the ends up and tie a knot at the top.

4. Fill the compartments with bird seed and hang your feeder in a tree.

Create your own confidence...

...by taking action to protect the planet.

28. Facing challenges

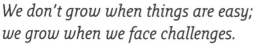

*We don't grow when things are easy;
we grow when we face challenges.*

— Unknown

Doing things you know you are good at
will make you feel confident and comfortable.

If you read books that are easy for you, it will be
enjoyable (but it won't make your reading better).

If you bake the same shortbread you have made
ten times before, everyone is sure to love it (but it
won't improve your baking skills).

Challenges can feel risky – there is a chance you
might fail, face obstacles, or feel uncomfortable.

BUT, if you challenge yourself to read harder books
you will discover amazing new stories.

Bake more complicated recipes and you could end
up making an amazing birthday cake.

Challenges push you forward and when you
succeed, the rewards are well worth the effort.
Your confidence will also get the biggest boost
from setting and achieving a new challenge.

How it works

Psychologist Carol Dweck discovered that success in any challenge is affected by our thinking.

She found that some people have a 'fixed mindset' – they didn't believe they could change their abilities so they would avoid challenges and stay stuck.

But she also found that some people had a 'growth mindset', and they believed their abilities could be *developed* so they tried hard.

Can you guess who got better results?

Activity: Challenge yourself

Can you think of a small challenge you could complete for a little trophy?

What about a medium-sized one for a bigger trophy?

And now let's aim high... what big challenge could you set yourself to win a HUGE trophy?

Create your own confidence...

...by approaching every challenge with a great attitude and hard work.

29. Build on your achievements

Self-confidence is the memory of success.
                                    - David Storey

Do you find it easier to talk about what went wrong rather than what went right? Maybe you think it's a bit boastful to celebrate.

It's important and helpful to think about, share and celebrate your achievements, big or small.

Maybe you improved your best swimming time or the speed of reciting the alphabet backwards or you beat your brother at chess for the first time ever. Your wins are precious. Hold on to them and don't be shy – share them with someone, give yourself a high five, you could even throw a party!

You can learn a lot from success. You can learn about hard work, being determined and having a great attitude. Remember what went well and carry it forward into what you do next.

How it works

The happy chemical dopamine is released in your brain when you achieve something, and it feels so good, you will want more of it and work hard to get that feeling again. So, focusing on your success encourages you to aim for more success!

Activity: Build on your success

Think about the questions below and keep a note of your answers so you can quickly look back on them if you ever need a confidence boost.

What have you done that you are proud of? There can be lots of examples here!

What took you ages to learn but you achieved in the end? What made you keep going?

Can you think of a time you achieved something that surprised you? How did that happen?

Create your own confidence...

...by giving your achievements lots of attention.

30. Marvellous mini goals

Dreams come a size too big so we can grow into them.
- Josie Bisset

Reaching a goal you have set yourself can feel amazing. It does wonders for your confidence because it helps you trust and believe in yourself and it makes you feel successful and skilled.

How it works

When you achieve something, your brain releases the feel-good hormone dopamine. Your body loves dopamine, it feels fabulous. So because you want to repeat that feeling again and again, you are motivated to achieve even more goals!

Breaking big goals into mini goals

Rather than set huge goals that would take ages and perhaps be really hard to meet, it is a good idea to break a big goal down into achievable mini goals that lead up, step by step, to the big one.

So, if you want to cycle 20 miles your mini goals might look like this:

1. Learn how to blow up tyres
2. Learn how to mend a puncture
3. Cycle around the block
4. Cycle 1 mile
5. Cycle 5 miles
6. Cycle 10 miles
7. Get sponsored
8. Do your 20-mile bike ride

Each time you achieve one of your goals, ticking it off the list will feel brilliant and you will be excited to move on to the next one.

Activity: Do it yourself!

With the help of your grown-up, come up with a list of tasks that you can do to help you feel more independent and increase your skills. Turn these tasks into a list of goals to be achieved.

Create your own confidence...

...by setting and achieving mini goals.

31. Problem-solving

Riddle: *When things go wrong,*
what can you always count on?

Answer: *Your fingers*

(Another answer that I like even better is... YOU!)

How good are you at solving problems?

Some people sit and think endlessly about what's wrong, not doing anything about it. Problem-dwelling can make a problem feel bigger than it is and cause extra unhappiness.

Talk then tackle

It is always good to think and talk about what's wrong but don't do this over and over. Moving onto problem-solving makes you feel that you are in control of your problem rather than it being in control of you. This makes you feel more confident.

The problem with not solving problems

Some children who don't have problem-solving skills act in ways that get them into trouble because they don't see that they have different choices.

Knowing how to solve a problem and remembering that you always have choices is the best way to make things better.

First, can you do anything at all about your problem?

No   Yes

If you are sure nothing can be done to solve your problem, try to stop worrying about it. Instead, fill your time with things that make you happy.

If yes, then BRILLIANT! That means there is an opportunity to practise your problem-solving skills.

Four simple steps to problem-solving

1. State your problem
2. Think of possible solutions
3. Explore which solution might work best
4. Pick one!

If step 4 doesn't work, pick another solution and try that instead. This four-step approach stops you being stuck. With practice it will become natural to approach problems like this rather than simply being upset by them.

What are these words anagrams of?

Melpobr   Rewsna

Can you find your way out of this maze?

Riddle time

I have a tail and a head, but no body.
What am I?

What two things can you never
eat for breakfast?

Create your own confidence...

...by becoming a great problem-solver.

colour me!

BODY CONFIDENCE

32. Power posing

Our bodies change our minds, and our minds can change our behaviour and our behaviour can change our outcomes.

- Amy Cuddy

Power poses are ways of standing that make you feel more confident and powerful.

You do them naturally when you feel confident, are leading or being a bit bossy!

When you stand a certain way, your body tells your mind that you are strong and prepared to face any challenge. (Your mind doesn't know if you are faking it!)

How it works

Amy Cuddy is a researcher in body language benefits. She says that if you stand for 2 minutes in any one of these 'high power' poses, it causes changes in hormone levels in your body, increasing testosterone (which helps you feel in control) and decreasing cortisol (which makes you feel stressed).

When your hormones tell your brain and body you aren't stressed and you are in control, your confidence soars.

Activity: Power poses

Try out these poses before doing something you find tricky and you will find you feel strong, powerful and capable.

Taking those feelings with you into any situation will help you look and feel more confident.

Let's take a look at four fabulous power poses on the next page. Try them all to find the one that works best for you.

With all of these poses stand straight, strong and tall. When we make ourselves big and take up more space, we feel stronger and more confident. This even works when we do it behind closed doors.

The victory pose

Raise your fists and arms above your head, keep your legs strong and slightly apart.

You see athletes do this a lot. It is the sign of a winner – which of course you are!

The Wonder Woman pose

Stand with your feet apart, chin lifted and your hands on your hips. You are a superhero.

The boss power pose

This pose is for when you are standing behind a table or desk at school.

Stand with your feet wide apart and put your hands down on the table on both sides of your body. Raise your chin up in the air.

Who is in control? You are!

The Superman pose

Plant your feet firmly about hip width apart.

Make a fist with one hand and then raise it in the air like Superman about to take off and perform a daring mission – then set off on your own brave adventure.

Create your own confidence...

...with power poses!

33. Body language

Never bend your head. Always hold it high.
Look the world straight in the eye.

— Helen Keller

Have you noticed that when you are feeling a bit fed up your shoulders slump and you look down at the ground? Or that when you feel unconfident you make yourself smaller, maybe wrapping your arms around yourself or scrunching your shoulders?

When you are happy you might throw your arms wide and smile brightly. When you are confident you probably stand up straighter, look people in the eye and put your shoulders back.

Your feelings show up in your body and this is your BODY LANGUAGE. It speaks for you even when no words come out of your mouth.

How it works

It's not just about body movements though – facial expressions, tone and volume of voice, and eye contact are all examples of body language. Some scientists say it makes up 80 percent of our communication. It gives people huge clues about what we are thinking and feeling.

Some of your own body language might happen without you even noticing (like tapping your fingers if you are impatient).

Our body language tells other people all sorts of things – if we are friendly, timid, angry, shy... and it speaks loudly about our confidence.

Scientists have found that just by changing our body language we can change how we feel.

One study from San Francisco University in America found that when people slouched, they usually felt sad and tired, but by purposefully sitting up they could improve their mood and energy.

Our mind gets signals from our body that change how we feel, so if you...

- smile – you will probably feel happier
- put your shoulders back – you could feel more confident
- use your hands to explain something – you might feel more enthusiastic.

Try changing how you feel by changing your body language.

Explore body language with this fun game.

Write the different emotions listed below on slips of paper. Can you think of any other emotions to add? then fold them up and put them into a bowl.

Take turns as a family or group of friends to pull a piece of paper out of the bowl and act out the emotion using body language for the rest of the group to guess.

excited

worried

frustrated

sad

ANGRY

stressed

CONFUSED

creative

happy

Create your own confidence...

...by learning about body language and using it to change how you feel.

34. Love your body

The minute you learn to love yourself, you won't want to be anyone else.

 - Rihanna

Do you love your body? I hope so because it is actually completely incredible.

Everyone's body is different – their shape, hair colour, physical abilities, skin colour, nose shape, eye colour...I could go on.

You have...

ears to hear	**eyes to see**
hands to write	**lips to speak**
nose to smell	bum to sit
knees to bend	**legs to walk**
arms to hug	**feet to stand**

It's amazing how different human beings can be.

Once we appreciate differences in others it is easier to be confident about what makes us unique.

How boring would the world be if everyone looked the same?

Body confidence

Some people don't feel confident about their body because they focus on what they can't do more than what they can. Sometimes, people don't like their body because they compare how they look to people they know or see on TV and then consider themselves less attractive.

Thinking this way can lead to a lack of confidence and it doesn't celebrate how amazing, beautiful and fabulous all bodies are!

It is a fact: every body is amazing, every body is different and every body deserves to be taken care of.

Your heart beats about 100,000 times a day. This means it pumps 2,000 gallons of blood around your body. Your body is just awe-inspiring (and busy!)..

Body image

Having a positive body image means that you feel comfortable with the way you look, and feel confident about what your body can do. It means you take care of your body with healthy food, exercise, good sleep and hygiene – and that occasionally you even brush your hair!

Activity: Appreciating every body

1. Think of five different people in your class or family and find something you appreciate about what their bodies can do or how they look.

1. _____

2. _____

3. _____

4. _____

5. _____

You might notice:

- Mum's warm hands that hold you tight
- Gran's springy purple hair
- Your baby brother's toothless smile

2. Next, take a look at your body and name five things you love about it.

1.

2.

3.

4.

5.

Think of all the amazing things your body enables you to do (like reading this book!).

Once you love your body you will hold your head high and smile more brightly – that makes everyone look more beautiful.

Create your own confidence...

...by loving your amazing body.

35. Love your brain

You have brains in your head. You have feet in your shoes. You can steer yourself any direction you choose.
- Dr Seuss

You should have lots of confidence in your brain as it helps you sleep, dream, think, create, learn, remember, move, feel, speak and form relationships!

Did you know...?

- It is about the same size as two fists and weights around 1,350 grams (the weight of a two-slice toaster).
- It is grey and made up of 60 percent fat.
- It oversees everything your body does, even breathing.
- It contains billions of cells that send and receive information through your body.

Just like your body, your brain needs nurturing to keep it in tip-top condition. This is what it likes:

1. Water. Don't go thirsty. Your brain won't work so well if you need a drink. It likes water best.

2. Exercise. Your memory improves with exercise and your brain needs your blood to be full of oxygen, so do exercise daily.

3. Sleep. Your brain loves a great night's sleep to process what you have learnt during the day and also to repair itself.

4. Food. Your brain likes you to eat well. Sugary snacks like chocolate aren't great for your brain. They release sugar so fast that your brain activity will peak but then quickly crash, making you feel tired. Your brain likes food that is rich in iron like spinach, dried fruit, cereals and pulses. And it loves baked beans.

Activity: Kiss your brain

Psychologist Christina Costa says every so often you should kiss your brain and say thank you.

Kiss your fingertips then touch them to your head and say thank you to your brain for helping you to solve that problem or access that beautiful memory or whatever it has done for you today.

Create your own confidence...

...by loving and looking after your awesome brain.

36. Listen to your body

Listen to your body. It is always communicating with you.
                                        - Unknown

Your body is a brilliant source of information and reacts quickly to your thoughts and feelings.

When you feel calm and confident your body is loose and relaxed and your breath slow and steady.

When you experience threatening situations (even just one you imagine) your clever brain prepares your body to fight, flight or freeze. Stress hormones flood your body and it gets ready for action. Your breathing quickens, your muscles tense, your face might get hot and your heart beats fast.

This can make your tummy hurt or your head ache, and it feels anything but relaxed!

What you think and feel has a huge effect on your body. And the opposite is also true. Your body – and what it's doing – affects your thoughts and feelings too. But the good news is that it's easy to take control of your body.

How it works

An important heart doctor called Herbert Benson discovered that people who practised relaxation had more peaceful minds and better health.

So, it follows that when we purposefully relax our bodies, our brains relax too. Dr Benson called this the *relaxation response* and suggested people practise relaxing their bodies daily.

Calm bodies and calm minds

Calm minds can focus better, they make better choices and decisions and they don't panic. Being calm is great for your confidence as it helps you feel more in control.

Anything you do to slow down your heartbeat and release tension in your muscles tells your brain everything is now okay and it can settle down.

Let's look at some great ways to relax your body and calm your emotions.

Activity: Relaxation bingo

Try and complete all the activities in the relaxation bingo. Score each body-relaxing activity out of ten for how well it calms your mind.

Imagine a candle. Take in a deep breath through your nose and then breathe out slowly through pursed lips as if you are trying to blow out the candle. Do this five times.	Walk in nature for at least 30 minutes.	Massage your hands with a little hand cream.
Listen to a calming piece of piano music.	Do a short yoga video.	Have a long, warm bath.
Snuggle into a soft, warm blanket.	Close your eyes and visualise walking along a beautiful beach.	Clench and release each of the muscles in your body, starting with your forehead down to your toes.

In the bubbles below, add some more ways you like to relax.

Create your own confidence...

...by relaxing your body to calm your mind.

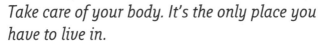

37. Exercise regularly

Take care of your body. It's the only place you have to live in.

- Jim Rohn

Exercise is a confidence booster!
Scientists have found that people who exercise regularly report increased feelings of confidence. They have linked this to the fact that exercising helps people develop their skills, a stronger body and better resilience (the ability to bounce back when things go wrong).

Skills
As you exercise regularly you will start to achieve more. Maybe you will run faster, walk further, do better tumbles.

Becoming more skilful at your sport will lead to feelings of pride and will give you confidence in your ability to learn new things and reach your goals.

A stronger body
With exercise, your physical fitness and strength will improve. When your body feels stronger, faster and healthier you will have more confidence to join in with games, join teams and try new sports.

Feeling confident in your body helps you feel confident in your mind, so do make sure you exercise regularly. It is recommended by the World Health Organisation that we all have 60 minutes of exercise every day.

Resilience

Resilience is your ability to get back up and try again. When you play sports and exercise you will fall off your bike, fall over on the ice, struggle with dance steps, miss a goal or climb back down the wall before you reach the top.

Learning to not give up when things go wrong is a great lesson for life. If you know you can cope with obstacles without being defeated, you will begin to develop trust and confidence in your body and in your mind.

Exercise is a mood booster

As well as all the above, when you do physical exercise your body produces chemicals in your brain called endorphins, which make you feel wonderful. So, if you are feeling a bit low in your mood, a little unconfident or worried, then a good dose of exercise is a great distraction and can change your mood.

Starting today, can you plan out (and complete) a week of exercise, being sure to try a couple of new things too?

Monday **Play frisbee**
Tuesday **Nature walk**
Wednesday **Family kitchen disco**
Thursday **Yoga**
Friday **Footie in the park**
Saturday **Skipping**
Sunday **Garden obstacle course**

What would your week look like?

Monday

Tuesday

Wednesday

Thursday

Friday

Saturday

Sunday

Create your own confidence...

...with daily exercise.

colour me!

SPEAKING WITH CONFIDENCE

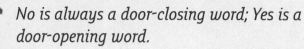

No is always a door-closing word; Yes is a door-opening word.

- Thomas Dreier

It can be tempting to say 'no' when someone suggests something that:

- scares you
- feels hard
- is uncomfortable.

Even if it seems super exciting (and safe), the thought of facing something tough can stop you saying 'yes'. This is a shame if the yes could have led to a fun and exciting opportunity.

Imagine your teacher asks you to take the lead in the school play and sing a solo. The thought terrifies you, so you say no. The night of the play comes, and you watch your friend in the spotlight instead, all eyes are on her and she has learnt to sing beautifully with so much practice. She is having the best time. You wish you had said yes.

Opportunities do not always arise again – or at least, not the same ones: so the school camp, tea at someone new's house, trying out for the netball team, that school play... You might not get another chance in the future.

Saying 'yes' opens doors – by saying yes to the school play you could be spotted and asked to be part of a local theatre group which might lead to a movie career in Hollywood (well, you never know!).

Dr Yes

Richard Branson is a businessman whose staff call him Dr Yes because he tries out lots and lots of adventurous activities, like trying to break the world speed record for crossing the Atlantic Ocean by boat. He failed but later did it in a hot-air balloon. Now he has set up a company to take people to space on holiday!

Sometimes he succeeds and sometimes he doesn't, and he is okay with that too. He says:

Life is a lot more fun when you say yes! It's amazing how that one little word can lead you on an incredible adventure.

Hannah's story

"Like my saxophone skills, my confidence grew gradually. On arrival at my secondary school, I goldfished (pretended to play) pretty much every note, sure that the rest of the band would play a different one.

Persistence pays. And so does practice. But it wasn't just my skills in sight reading I needed to develop. I lacked the mindset to get out there and perform. I preferred to stay in my bedroom, but my teacher had other ideas for me. With his help I pushed myself out of my shell and my section. First with bands. Then with busking. Rural outreach projects led to an audition for a national jazz summer school. It was hard, but I was up for it, spending a residential week in the Midlands.

I knew the notes would sound okay this time and that my new skills and confidence would come through for me. On a zoom call with Prince Edward, Earl of Wessex, in lockdown, I wasn't afraid to express myself. I might still prefer my bedroom but I'm definitely not a goldfish any more.

With time and support confidence can grow – you just need to say 'yes.' "

Think of one thing you would like to be able to say 'yes' to, but you feel unconfident about.

Write it down as a goal in the centre of a blank page.

Now fill that page with things that support that YES by listing...

- the people who could help you
- the positive and encouraging words you could tell yourself
- the talent and skills which make that yes possible
- the things you could gain from trying it

...then go for it!

(Your yes might not work out but tell yourself loud and clear that you can cope either way, because you can. And who knows, your YES might just lead to amazing things!)

Create your own confidence...

...by saying a confident YES to adventures and opportunities.

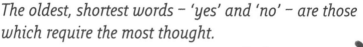

39. Say NO with confidence

The oldest, shortest words – 'yes' and 'no' – are those which require the most thought.

- Pythagoras

You always have the right to say 'no'.

If you are being told it is time to get up for school or to do your chores, saying 'no' will probably get you told off. It is important to not say 'no' just because you can't be bothered.

But (and this is important) sometimes your 'no' will really matter and will keep you and others safe and on the right path, such as when someone asks you to do something you believe is wrong, dangerous or unkind.

At times like this, you need to be able to say 'no' with confidence.

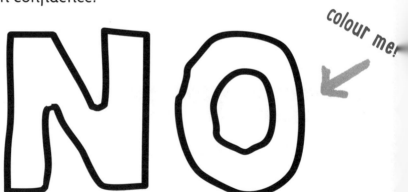

colour me!

Why is saying 'no' so hard?

Dr Vanessa Bohns, a science professor at the University of Waterloo in Canada, has discovered the fear of saying 'no' sometimes comes from a wish to avoid arguments or confrontations. Other times, she suggests, people worry about saying 'no' because they don't want to disappoint others or hurt their feelings.

Have you ever done this?

It can be far easier to say 'yes' than 'no' to a bossy friend or to an adult who makes you feel nervous or uncomfortable. Just because something is easy though, doesn't mean it is right or the best decision for you.

Saying 'no' can be hard, but sometimes being able to do so matters (a lot) and the more you do it the more comfortable you will be with it. You need to practise in order to say 'no' with confidence.

Activity: Role play

Have a look at the questions below. Once you have decided on your answer, have a go at role playing the scenario with your friend or grown-up.

1. A boy at school asks you to come to his house for a sleepover but you really don't want to go. You don't like him very much and none of your other friends are going.

What would you say?

- Er, okay, yes. Thanks for asking me.
- I'll have to check my diary and get back to you.
- No, thanks for asking but I am not able to make it.

2. Your best friend announces to your friendship group that you should ignore the new kid at school because 'she looks weird'.

What would you say?

- Yes, good idea!
- No, I'm not prepared to do that.
- No, I want to make her feel welcome.

The only wrong answer is saying 'yes' when you know it should be a 'no'.

The more we practise saying no when we need to, the easier it will be.

3. Can you think of your own example below ?

_____

_____

_____

_____

Create your own confidence...

...by saying NO when you know you should.

40. Public speaking

I've learned that people will forget what you said, people will forget what you did, but people will never forget how you made them feel.
- Maya Angelou

Some people are happy to put their hand up in class to answer a question or to read something that they have written in front of everyone in assembly.

For others, speaking publicly is terrifying and they either use a tiny voice when they do, or they avoid it completely.

Researchers say that one in every four people struggle with public speaking. If this applies to you don't worry, speaking in public with confidence is something you can learn.

Speak up, we can't hear you at the back!
Speaking comfortably in front of others makes school easier and will come in handy later when you have a job interview or a presentation at work. It also makes other things easier such as drama or singing on stage.

Fear of public speaking is also known as
glossophobia or *stage fright*.

It might make you shake or feel sick, your heart
might race and you want to run away. This is
because your amygdala (the emotion processor in
your brain) hears your fear and gives your body the
message to get ready for 'fight or flight'.

The changes in your body and brain make it
difficult for you to think clearly and you might
completely forget what you have to say.

Good news
The more you practise public speaking, the more
confidence you will have, and this will start to
squash your fear. The better you get at public
speaking, the less scared you will be because the
thinking part of your brain will kick in and say I
CAN do this.

Activity: Four steps to public speaking

1. Pick a story and read it aloud slowly and clearly without an audience. Remember to pause and breathe and put expression into the words.

2. Now try reading it in front of a parent or a good friend. Be brave and ask them for any helpful feedback they can give you.

3. Now try again, standing at the back of a room and talking more loudly. Stand up tall and smile as you talk. This will make you look (and feel) more confident.

4. Repeat steps 1 to 3 but instead of reading from a book, talk about your favourite hobby for 2 minutes.

By the end of these steps, you will have greater confidence and be more skilled at public speaking. Next time you have to do it you can truthfully tell yourself, 'I know how to do this', and you will find that you can.

Keep finding new ways to improve your confidence in public speaking. Can you think of some other things you can do to keep practising? Write these on the next page.

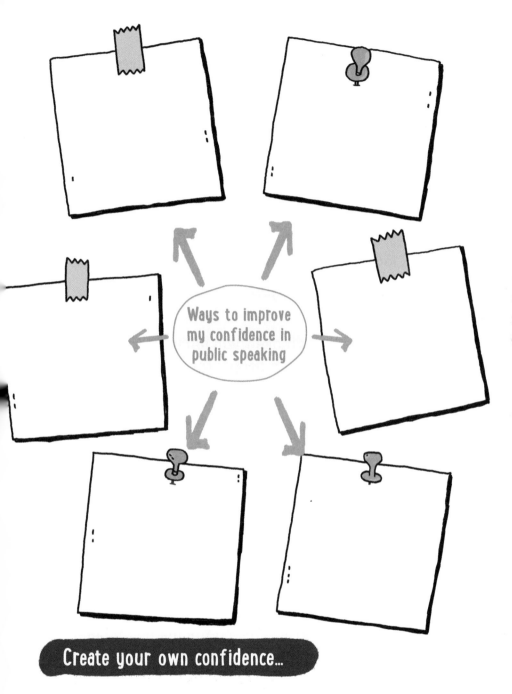

Ways to improve my confidence in public speaking

Create your own confidence...

...by learning to speak up.

41. Accepting compliments

On a scale from 1 to 10, you're an 11.

Some people just love compliments. They see them as little gifts and adore hearing things like:

- You are kind.
- I love your smile.
- You make me laugh.

Such compliments make them smile and say, 'Thank you'. And when people take compliments on board, they feel more confident.

Not everyone responds like this
If you struggle to accept a compliment and feel embarrassed by it, it might be because you are shy or get a bit nervous when the spotlight is on you.

You might also struggle to accept a compliment because you don't think you deserve it or believe it can be true.

But if you listen closely, the compliment can help your confidence rise.

Give them away

One way to get used to compliments is to give more away. A compliment costs nothing but is worth gold to the receiver. Getting used to giving compliments and seeing the joy they bring will help you accept them more easily too.

Just say 'thank you'

Sometimes other people notice wonderful things about you that you just don't see. You don't have to agree with them, but don't disagree either – they are just sharing their opinion. All you need to say is, 'Thank you'.

How it works

Scientists have found that accepting compliments activates the same part of your brain that lights up when you receive money.

Compliments can make you feel amazing!

Activity: Make a compliments jar

Grab a jar and stick a label on the front with COMPLIMENTS written on it.

Every time someone gives you a compliment, write it on a scrap of paper and pop it into your jar. If you are having a bad day, pull one out to reread. Reading it again will warm your heart and build your confidence.

Compliment yourself when you are pleased with yourself and add those compliments to your jar too. Saying good things to yourself boosts your confidence and makes it easier to believe that other people's compliments are true.

Why not try to compliment yourself right now? In the space on the right, right three things you are good at.

colour me!

Compliments Jar

1. _____

_____

_____

2. _____

_____

_____

3. _____

_____

_____

Create your own confidence...

...by accepting any compliments you are given.

42. Asking for help

Don't be shy about asking for help. It doesn't mean you're weak, it only means you're wise.
                              - Unknown

Do you have the confidence to ask for help? You might feel shy or uncomfortable or you might be concerned that the person you're asking to help you will think you are needy, annoying or stupid.

Courage is a muscle – it gets stronger every time we use it. So, each time you ask for help, it will get easier, and you will feel more comfortable about it.

How it works

Psychologist Heidi Grant found that people are almost 50 percent more likely to want to help than you think they are (so make sure you always ask for the help you need!).

There is an interesting theory called the Ben Franklin effect that shows people will often like you more when you have asked them for a favour (so asking for help can be a good way to make friends!).

Asking for help can make everyone feel good

When we ask for and receive help it can make us feel closer to others and help us to learn new things.

Asking for help from someone tells them that you think they have skills, that they are kind and that you trust them.

Activity: List your helpers

Draw a picture of yourself holding six big balloons. At the top of each balloon, write a heading from the list below.

Physical health (being fit and healthy)

Emotional health (feeling calm and happy)

Education (learning at school and tests)

Skills (hobbies and independence skills)

Friendships (making friends, bullying and arguments)

Confidence (loving and believing in yourself)

In each balloon, write in the names of people you could ask for help in these areas of your life.

Create your own confidence...

...by asking for help when you need it.

43. Encourage yourself

You yourself, as much as anybody in the entire universe, deserve your love and affection
— Brené Brown

How you SPEAK to yourself has a huge impact on your confidence, so you need to speak to yourself with words of kindness and positivity.

Think about it

How do you feel if someone tells you off, says something mean to you or criticises you?

The chances are you'll feel rubbish. No one likes to hear mean words, put-downs or be spoken to angrily. It knocks your confidence and upsets you.

So why would you do this to yourself?

You can't choose what other people say to you but you can ALWAYS choose the words you say to yourself. Speak to yourself like you are your own biggest fan, cheerleader and coach and your confidence will bloom.

Affirmations are positive phrases we can say to ourselves to help banish unhelpful thoughts. Researchers have found that they lower stress and stop us worrying so much too.

If you practise saying confidence affirmations, your brain will find it easier to use them when you begin to talk to yourself in a negative way. They can help to turn your thoughts around quickly.

Here are some to get you started:

I can do this.

I believe in myself.

I will do my best.

Activity: Affirmations poster

Make a poster of confidence-boosting affirmations. You could use the affirmations in the list and add in some of your own too. Put the poster up somewhere you will see it often.

Create your own confidence…

…by encouraging yourself and practising your affirmations.

44. Assertiveness

If you don't ask, the answer is always no.
- Nora Roberts

Asking for what you want in a clear, calm manner is called being assertive. This is your best chance of getting what you want as it is polite, and your wishes are easy to understand.

Confident people ask for what they want. They believe they have a right to be heard.

Assertiveness is powerful

Assertive kids do things like...

- putting up their hand and asking for help in class,

- telling their friends how they feel if they get teased by them, and

- saying if they really don't like being hugged, even if it might hurt someone's feelings.

Being assertive makes your life better even if it feels like a scary thing to do at first.

Three steps to assertiveness

1. Use the word 'I'. Say clearly how you feel and what you would like to happen.

2. If they say no, you could try again.

3. If being assertive still doesn't work, think about what else you could do to get your needs met. (Perhaps walk away, or ask someone else to help you?)

Activity: Role play

A great way to practise assertiveness is to role play it. Rope in a friend or a family member and try out these scenarios.

1. Your friend has taken your ball in the middle of a game of cricket. She is just laughing and won't give it back. What do you do?

2. Your dad wants you to go to his friend's house for tea on the same day as your best friend's birthday party. How will you tell him 'no'?

_____

_____

_____

_____

_____

3. Your teacher sets you some science homework and you don't understand what she wants you to do. What could you say?

_____

_____

_____

_____

_____

Remember to breathe slowly and deeply before you act out your scenes, to help you feel calm. Afterwards, chat over how they went.

Create your own confidence

...by practising being assertive.

colour me!

CONFIDENCE IN RELATIONSHIPS

45. The confidence squad

Alone we can do so little; together we can do so much.
— Helen Keller

It always feels lovely to be supported and appreciated. Building a confidence squad creates a team of people who lift you up rather than put you down.

Listen to how you feel
Spend your time with people who help you feel more confident by reassuring you when you are feeling unsure and cheering you on if you are having a wobble. These people will remind you that you are fabulous, that you can do it and that they are there for you if things don't work out.

Stay close to the people who make you feel like your best self. Perhaps that includes cousins or a grandparent, certain friends, a coach, a teacher, a parent or a sibling. They may have nothing to do with each other, but you'll know they're all on your side.

How to build your team
Invest a lot of your time and energy in supporting your fabulous, confidence-boosting teammates

and making your relationships even stronger. Give compliments, support, encouragement, praise and time to the people who give it to you.

If you need some more teammates, try to spread your friendship circle at breaktimes or through hobbies or clubs, and be a great confidence-booster yourself.

It doesn't matter how many people are in your team as long as your teammates are good to you, and you are good to them.

Activity: Pick your squad

Imagine you were putting together a list of players for your confidence team. Your players can be any age or level of fitness for this team. They just need one talent: they need to make you feel confident about who you are.

Your team list can be as big as you wish. Who makes your squad? Keep your team close.

Create your own confidence...

...by surrounding yourself with warm people and not worrying about the 'cool' people.

46. Standing up and speaking out

Unless someone like you cares a whole awful lot, nothing is going to get better. It's not.

— The Lorax

Do you find it easy to stand up for yourself or for others? How about speaking out about things you believe in?

It can be tricky to speak up sometimes; you might fear annoying someone or worry it will get you into trouble. You might be embarrassed for the spotlight to be on you.

Many things can stop you speaking out when you want to. Let's take a look at what could help.

Know your WHY

If you are clear about why you need to speak up, you will have more confidence in what you want to say.

Practise

When you have to do something that is hard and you are nervous or embarrassed, practising can help.

SAVE THE HEDGEHOG

Get support

When you aren't sure how best to take a stand, getting support and guidance can be a big help. For example...

- If you want to march against climate change, you could ask your family if they want to join in and you could make placards together.

- If you want to stand up to someone who is bossing you around at school, you could ask your friends to stand by your side.

- If you want to support your friend who is being bullied, you could ask them (or your teacher) what kind of support would be best.

Activity: Say it loud!

Make a banner or a placard to promote a cause you believe in.

Maybe you could ask your teacher if your cause could become a class topic, or you could even write to your MP about it.

Create your own confidence...

...by speaking out about what you believe in.

47. Not following the crowd

You must never be fearful about what you are doing when it is right.

- Rosa Parks

Following the crowd means doing what others do. People usually do this because they want to be liked and accepted and because it feels safe.

To not follow the crowd means to go in a different direction and make your own choices.

How it works

Psychologists call the tendency people have to do something because everyone else is doing it *the bandwagon effect*, as people usually 'jump on the bandwagon' (which means they copy everyone else).

They found that even usually tidy people are more likely to litter if they're in an environment that's littered.

Even though it might feel scary going your own way, it increases your confidence because you learn to depend on YOURSELF not others. It teaches you to trust yourself.

Sometimes it is easy to do your own thing but not always.

If you practise acting independently on the things that don't matter so much (such as hair styles), then when things do matter, you will be prepared.

What matters?

- If your friends are doing something unsafe or unkind, it's important not to join in.
- If you have a dream or believe in something, it's important not to walk away from it.

Sometimes you are going to have to trust that voice in you that says, 'I think what I am doing is right.'

Activity: Time for a chat

What do you do, or think or believe, that is different to most of your friends?

Talk about this with someone you trust and let your feelings flow. Listen to how much you care and how passionate you feel. This will encourage you to follow your own path.

Create your own confidence...

...by not always following the crowd.

48. Making friends

In the cookie of life, friends are the chocolate chips.

- Unknown

Friendships are lovely – having friends means having someone to support you, cheer you on, and tell you daft jokes. Good friends are fantastic.

Did you know...?

Creating close friendships can take some time. A recent study at the University of Kansas in America found that it takes about 50 hours of socialising to go from just being someone you know to being a casual friend, another 40 hours for someone to become a 'real' friend, and a total of 200 hours of hanging out together for someone to become a close friend.

Activity: Be the friend you want to have

Write a list of five things you want in a friend and then commit to being those five things yourself.

If you are confident that you have all the qualities of a good friend yourself, you will know for sure that people will enjoy your friendship.

```
V  P  K  S  O  V  G  I  R  T  D  W  V  U  C
B  T  X  L  U  W  K  V  A  G  H  U  N  D  W
U  Y  Q  N  O  P  W  P  T  S  C  P  N  S  A
T  L  Y  C  G  Y  P  Z  T  P  F  B  W  W  R
H  R  H  N  G  I  A  O  D  Z  Z  E  T  F  M
O  S  W  O  J  X  V  L  R  X  F  U  N  G  P
U  T  S  M  I  L  E  I  M  T  H  G  W  O  M
G  E  N  E  R  O  U  S  N  V  I  T  P  E  D
H  O  V  Z  P  A  Z  O  K  G  C  V  H  S  G
T  E  N  C  O  U  R  A  G  I  N  G  E  R  Q
F  Z  J  Q  J  S  F  R  I  E  N  D  L  Y  T
U  S  R  P  N  V  Q  D  K  J  C  K  I  N  D
L  J  U  O  C  Z  O  V  T  I  K  A  O  B  L
R  V  L  O  F  M  P  T  U  L  D  M  K  V  F
I  F  R  I  E  N  D  S  H  I  P  O  E  N  Y
```

ENCOURAGING	SUPPORTIVE	FRIENDLY	GENEROUS
GIVING	FRIENDSHIP	LOYAL	SMILE
KIND	WARM	FUN	THOUGHTFUL

Have a look at the wordsearch above. Can you find
any words that go with being a good pal?

Create your own confidence...

...by reaching out and making new friends.

49. Feeling shy

The way you overcome shyness is to become so wrapped up in something that you forget to be afraid.
- Lady Bird Johnson

Shyness can feel a bit like fear; it can make you tremble or blush and it can make your heart race. It's an uncomfortable feeling that might make you want to hide or run away, and it can affect your confidence.

Did you know...?

Over 50 percent of people say they are shy. This means people are more likely to understand and support you if you explain that you are feeling shy, because most likely they know how it feels too.

How it works

Scientists have discovered that 15 percent of babies are born with a tendency towards shyness. But even if you were born shy there are still things you can do to overcome it because of your brain's neuroplasticity (which simply means the ability your brain has to change and grow the more you practise something).

Five ways to overcome shyness

1. Choose an affirmation (a positive statement) like 'I can handle this' and repeat it silently in your head when you feel shy.

2. Wear a big smile. It helps others to see you are warm and friendly.

3. Rehearse your opening line. Knowing what you are going to say first stops you feeling panicky.

4. Think about when you have been shy before but then had an amazing time.

5. Realise it is okay to feel awkward but to do it anyway. Don't let feeling shy stop you.

Activity: So much more than shy

Think of ten positive words that other people use to describe you (ask them if you are struggling to think of any).

Make a list of these words and keep it safe.

When you are facing a new situation read this list beforehand. Remind yourself you are so much more than shy.

Create your own confidence...

...by taking control of your shyness.

50. Shine your light

Never let anyone or anything distract you from noticing how amazing you are.

— Edmond Mbiaka

You can create your own confidence by applying all you have learnt in this little book to your life and by practising again and again until it becomes easy.

I hope you have learnt that you should take pride in being an individual, that you are strong, that you know how to make friends, problem-solve, deal with failure and create and achieve goals.

Mostly I hope by now you realise you have every right to feel confident, because you truly are one-of-a-kind AMAZING.

When other people see your confidence shine, through your beaming smile and your positive actions, I know they will also see just how absolutely amazing you are too.

Science tells us that confidence is catching, so when you shine your light brightly everyone around you will glow a little brighter too.

Shine on!